5s for Healthcare

By Ade Asefeso MCIPS MBA

Copyright 2014 by Ade Asefeso MCIPS MBA
All rights reserved.

Second Edition

ISBN-13: 978-1499398106
ISBN-10: 1499398107

Publisher: AA Global Sourcing Ltd
Website: http://www.aaglobalsourcing.com

Table of Contents

Disclaimer 5
Dedication 6
Chapter 1: Introduction 7
Chapter 2: Why Use Lean Tools in Healthcare? .. 11
Chapter 3: How to Begin Thinking About 5s 15
Chapter 4: 5s Mindset 19
Chapter 5: Improvement Methodology for Healthcare Processes 25
Chapter 6: Starting 5s Lean in Your Healthcare Organization 27
Chapter 7: Implementing 5s Lean in Your Healthcare Organization 33
Chapter 8: Why 5s Lean Matters and How It's Done 37
Chapter 9: Turn Your Waiting Room Into a 5s Lean Showcase 41
Chapter 10: 5s Lean Help You Stay Profitable 45
Chapter 11: 5s Lean Culture and Wheelchair Inventory Control 49
Chapter 12: Disciplined Daily Management System 53
Chapter 13: Waste Reduction 55
Chapter 14: Status at a Glance 59
Chapter 15: Tracking the Right Metrics 63
Chapter 16: Red Tag Process in Lean Healthcare 67

Chapter 17: Airport Analogy as a Great Example of Simplicity 69
Chapter 18: Eliminating Some of the Built in Waste 71
Chapter 19: Leadership in a Lean Healthcare Environment 75
Chapter 20: 5s Reduce Financial Pressure 79
Chapter 21: Success Factors for 5s 83
Chapter 22: The Sixth S 87
Chapter 23: Conclusion 89

Disclaimer

This publication is designed to provide competent and reliable information regarding the subject matter covered. However, it is sold with the understanding that the author and publisher are not engaged in rendering professional advice. The authors and publishers specifically disclaim any liability that is incurred from the use or application of contents of this book.

If you purchased this book without a cover you should be aware that this book may have been stolen property and reported as "unsold and destroyed" to the publisher. In this case neither the author nor the publisher has received any payment for this "stripped book."

Dedication

This book is dedicated to the hundreds of thousands of incredible souls in the world who have weathered through the up and down of recent recession.

To my family and friends who seems to have been sent here to teach me something about who I am supposed to be. They have nurtured me, challenged me, and even opposed me.... But at every juncture has taught me!

This book is dedicated to my lovely boys, Thomas, Michael and Karl. Teaching them to manage their finance will give them the lives they deserve. They have taught me more about life, presence, and energy management than anything I have done in my life.

Chapter 1: Introduction

There are a variety of techniques and tools available to achieve the objectives associated with Lean Thinking. Lean, however, is not simply a set of tools. Lean is a problem solving approach for continuous daily improvement. Lean is about creating increased value for your customers (patients) by eliminating wasteful activities. Any activity or process that consumes resources or adds cost or time without creating value is a target for elimination.

One of the important aspects of Lean is the focus on "service-level" improvements. Think in terms of value-stream improvements (e.g. outpatient surgery or inpatient obstetrical care value streams). Improvements made along an entire value stream or service will result in increased efficiency, improved quality, and increased safety with dramatic cost savings.

The following are key points of Lean Thinking that you must not lose sight of if you are going to be successful in its application:
1. Each employee will arrive at work everyday thinking about how they are going to improve their work environment; with this commitment, there is continuous daily improvement.
2. Measurement is essential. Understanding the value stream baseline and the subsequent improvement achieved is critical. Measurement is key to continuous

improvement and provides a basis for understanding your accomplishments.

If you are thinking of implementing a 5s Lean process strategy in your healthcare facility; smart move, because hospitals today face the dilemma of providing continued levels of service quality, patient safety and security at lesser costs.

The five steps of 5s Lean; **Sort, Set in order, Shine, Standardize, and Sustain** are a proven effective method to help facilities organize workspaces to become inherently more presentable, productive, and safe. Each one provides essential activities that eliminate issues such as compliance and cleanliness, inventory control, and productivity. And learning these five steps is the first step in "going lean."

Sort: Sorting separates all that is necessary from the unnecessary. The quarantined collection of all unnecessary items is then discarded or placed in a designated area with other infrequently used items.

Set in Order: Setting all things in order prevents difficulties in searching and opens up spaces for more storage.

Shine: Shining is, in other words, a thorough cleaning process. It involves locating and eliminating sources of un-cleanliness or contamination, in addition to the sanitation of all spaces. This is vital for healthcare facilities in the fight to prevent in-hospital infections from occurring.

Standardize: Standardizing the system utilizes placement of visual cues and other strategies to make the process of sorting, setting in order, and shining uniform throughout a facility.

Sustain: Sustaining the system is the last step and arguably most difficult in accomplishing. When achieved, sustaining the 5s system becomes habitual and creates a restless sense when things are out of order.

As you begin to put together your 5s Lean plan, remember, 5s is not a project. It is a mindset that should be carried out with designed purpose and in a manner that includes every able individual. It is small changes, not just big ones that will help your facility, clinic, or clinical lab become a more functional, clean, and satisfying place for both personnel and patients.

Chapter 2: Why Use Lean Tools in Healthcare?

Healthcare costs are increasing more rapidly than costs for other products and services. Healthcare providers, particularly hospitals, are under significant pressure to reduce costs while at the same time improving service and patient safety, reducing patient waiting times, and minimizing errors and associated litigation. However, most hospitals are not making the necessary improvements in cost, quality, and safety. 20 percent of consecutive inpatient stays were associated with poor quality care, unnecessary fragmentation of care, or both.

Healthcare organizations, historically, have not been designed to make service processes or a "value stream" of care flow. Healthcare services often use a "batch and queue" process, with patients spending the bulk of their time waiting until a health care professional is ready (i.e., push versus pull with regard to service delivery).

Patient cycle time (the total time from the beginning to the end of a process) in our hospitals, laboratories, and therapy settings becomes a key measurement that needs to improve.

All types of organizations are leveraging Lean principles and tools. Many organizations are trying to function effectively in the face of growing challenges such as a high costs, declining market share, and limited capacity. In all of these cases, Lean can have an immediate, positive impact on business.

Healthcare organizations are made up of a series of processes with diverse services or lines of business. Therefore, you need to build delivery systems with these lines of business in mind. Using Lean Thinking, your organization can achieve a number of benefits, which may include improved quality, increased operational flexibility, reduced cycle time within processes, more efficient use of space, consistent service delivery, reduced lead times, and reduced operating costs.

Lean Tools: 5s

Lean tools grew out of the need to have mechanisms in place to support the lean way of thinking and to allow flow to permeate a process. Value stream mapping, 5s, Poka Yoke, and Kanban are among the most popular Lean tools.

The five components of 5s are defined as sort, set in order, shine, standardize, and sustain. 5s is a method that reduces waste in your work environment through better workplace organization, visual communication, and general cleanliness.

This is one of the primary tools necessary to improve your processes by eliminating wastes such as motion, searching, inventory (queuing) and improve quality and functionality within all departments.

5s Benefits

5s drives a cleaner work environment and organizes the workplace. It is a Lean tool that should be implemented along with process improvements identified when value-stream mapping your business processes. When implementing 5s, you rapidly affect your work or production environment with a minimal expenditure. Most organizations report 5-10% efficiency improvement in several months, which is sustainable over time. 5s provides some of the following benefits:

1. A cleaner workplace for enhanced safety and reduced clutter.
2. An organized, efficient workplace for increased productivity.
3. An always-ready environment that fosters and promotes compliance with regulatory standards.
4. The reduction of inventory and supply costs.
5. The recapture of valuable space and minimizing overhead costs.
6. The impact of "how we feel" about our workplace, organization, and ourselves.

There will be naysayers that may argue that their messiness is beneficial to them; some point to the fact that time spent keeping their environment organized distracts from the important things in their jobs like time analyzing or thinking and defining new approaches to care.

However, they miss the point; truly organized people are not organized just for the sake of order. Instead, their organization is a result of having a process to manage all of the things in their lives. These folks avoid the repeated distraction paper or e-mails in their inbox by having a clear approach for handling all of the responsibilities in their lives. By managing things effectively, they avoid clutter and chaos.

Chapter 3: How to Begin Thinking About 5s

When implementing 5s, staff should not focus on getting organized. Rather, they need to consider how they deal with all the things that come to them and what is within their environment; this will help in creating a 5s workplace. For example, doctors do not focus on getting their operating room organized. Instead, they have a defined process for preparing for an operation: they wash their hands in a certain way; the instruments used are predefined and laid out in a specific way. Instruments are checked and counted in a standard way for each surgical case every day. The result of these processes is a 5s workplace.

Let us use the practical example of cleaning your garage to understand how you would implement 5s in the workplace. The first step that you do when cleaning your garage is open the door, back out the cars, and pull everything out that is lying around. You then make piles of the things you will keep, what you will sell in the neighbourhood garage sale, items you need to return to a neighbour, what to donate, and what to discard. This first step in the process is called **"Sort."**

The next step is to put away the things that you wish to keep. However, this time you will put them in a specific location: "A place for everything and everything in its place." You make a shadow board for your tools. This will allow you and others to look at the board in the future and know exactly what location to return the tool to, and you can easily identify missing tools by the shape of the empty space on the board. More importantly, it allows you to find your tools when needed. You install hooks for bicycles in the ceiling joints and clamps for brooms and shovels. This step in the process is called **"Set in order."**

With everything sorted and set in order, it is time to clean the entire garage. When you are cleaning, you observe things that need to be fixed, such as the cracked switch plate and the torn weather stripping on the utility door. You repair these things so that they do not become a bigger problem, cause damage, or put a family member's safety at risk. Further, you hose down the garage floor and remove oil spills with a degreasing agent. This step is called **"Shine."**

Now you can stand back and look at your accomplishment. The garage looks great. Everything is clean and organized; you can actually find what you are looking for in the garage. However, beware you will need to repeat this exercise again in a few months because you did not **"Standardize" and "Sustain"** your efforts. Standardizing means to create the guidelines for Sort, Set in order, and Shine and then to actually follow those guidelines.

Sustain is having the discipline and keeping the 5s processes going. By implementing all of the 5s components, you have transformed your garage into a neat, orderly, and safe place. Everyone can find things quickly, and you can easily recognize when something is missing. This simple example reveals the power of 5s and the importance of using all of the 5s steps to move your Lean efforts forward.

5s is an integral part of the Lean Healthcare process which promotes "A Place for Everything and Everything is in its Place". When 5s is performed as the first step of a Lean Healthcare effort, processes become more visible and identified "waste" is cleaned out. While change is often perceived with a sense of apprehension, participants in the 5s program begin to taste change as something that can be positive and even fun, paving the way for a true Lean Healthcare transformation. 5s clearly communicates that management is willing to allow the employees to be involved in the process of change. The goal of the program is to have a workstation and office area that is Joint Commission ready at all times. 5s creates a neat, clean and orderly environment that will become a source of lasting pride for all employees.

The benefits of Healthcare 5s implementation as part of a Lean Healthcare initiative includes:
- An organized, efficient workplace for improved productivity.
- A cleaner workplace for improved safety and less clutter.
- Reducing inventory and supply costs.
- Recapturing valuable floor space and minimizing overhead costs.
- Contributes to "how we feel" about our service, our facility, and ourselves.

- Provides an always-ready showcase to promote compliance.

Chapter 4: 5s Mindset

The challenges healthcare organizations world-wide faced are consistent every year despite which country's healthcare legislation of the moment dominates the news.

How do we provide the highest quality care at the lowest possible cost?

There are an endless number of opinions about how to reach these goals simultaneously. One mindset that has contributed to improved health outcomes, better financial results, and boosted patient and staff satisfaction scores, is 5s Lean.

5s Lean is an organizational system that originated in manufacturing. It's been used across the globe for several decades. Innovative minds in healthcare leadership have borrowed and applied the 5s mindset since the 1990's. When healthcare leaders understand, and communicate to their staff, that 5s Lean is a continuous mindset, not a short-term project, they have been able to create impressive success stories.

Sort

Separate the necessary from the unnecessary; the frequently-used from the less frequently-used. Designate space for the high-frequency medical supplies. Make it accessible and as convenient as possible for your staff. Relegate the less frequently used supplies to a space that does not encroach on the highly valued space that should be set aside for the high use, most-important items. Sort should be a continuous process, and should be done in as little time as possible.

Set In Order

Now that you have set aside space and sorted and separated your frequently used from your infrequently used supplies, you will start the next stage of organization; set your medical supplies in order. It is time to get specific with how and where you will store these items.

Assign a specific, permanent, and easily accessible location for each type of medical supply. (Note: I use the word "permanent" here so that staff will always know where to find what they are looking for, even when they are stressed-out, tired, and rushed, these are all too common conditions in medical care. That said, "Permanent" does not mean that the storage location cannot or should not be moved when an opportunity to improve the storage and its location arises. Allow improvements to happen. That is welcome change. Think of "permanent" as a location that staff can depend on to find what they need.

Define what quantities of each supply should be in that location and what is the minimum quantity that will trigger re-stocking. In manufacturing, these are known as "par-levels" and this terminology has transferred to healthcare materials management in many circles.

Organize medical supplies in parallel and perpendicular order for easy access and to reduce the chance of grabbing the wrong item. Give each item set boundary with shelves, bins or drawer organizers for example. Develop an easy and obvious labelling system for everything you store. Labels should be easily read. Many organizations have found that introducing a colour-coding system to their storage has helped a great deal. Always look for ways to simplify and improve your sorting system.

Shine

Maintain a clean work space and storage space. Cleanliness has many benefits in healthcare:
- It reduces the spread of bacteria, viruses, and infectious diseases in your healthcare facility.
- Patient and staff health and safety improves.
- The facility becomes more attractive to the patients and families who use your facility and its services, which can boost your Hospital Consumer Assessment of Healthcare Providers and Systems (HCAHPS) formal public reporting scores.

(Note: in the US HCAHPS asks patients to rate their experiences regarding their inpatient stay. The ratings are shared with the public and can impact a healthcare organization's reputation in the community as well the amount it will be reimbursed for services provided to Medicare patients.)

Standardize

Now formalize the responsibilities, the space allocation, the par-levels, the organization system, and the cleaning requirements for your organization. In short, "standardize" your "sort", "set in order", and "shine" activities so that they happen on a consistent basis. Everyone involved should understand their specific responsibilities in these processes. The most successful organizations, not only in healthcare but also in manufacturing where 5s was perfected, use visual aids to quickly and accurately alert employees to standards compliance.

Sustain

The fifth "S", "sustain", can make or break your efforts. Your team has invested time and effort, and no doubt money, to sort, set in order, shine, and standardize. What a shame if they do not have a plan to sustain it in the long-term. This is why 5s Lean is considered a "mindset" and not a short-term project. It is a way of thinking about how you will operate your organization so that it provides the highest-quality medical care at the least possible expense.

From 2003 till now, the top-ranking concerns of healthcare CEOs have been financial challenged, followed by patient safety and quality of care, according to the American College of Healthcare Executives' (ACHE's) annual survey of issues confronting hospitals.

While many have adopted the 5s Lean mindset in their healthcare organizations, many more have yet to understand how they can realize the same return on investment that the manufacturing industry has shown.

If you are a healthcare leader needing to persuade your staff to make the effort and investment in the 5s Lean mindset, there are ways you can draw correlations from their investment to returns in finance, quality of care, and patient safety.

The 5s culture is a commitment to bring order to work, and reduce wastefulness found in operations and management. In healthcare this translates readily to organized storage of medical supplies, making them easily accessible by healthcare staff where and when they need them.

Chapter 5: Improvement Methodology for Healthcare Processes

Sustain: Perhaps the most challenging part of the 5s mindset, but when achieved, also the most rewarding. Employees committed to sustaining their efforts will feel restless when they find something out of order. Success at this stage means people will self-regulate the process and the order they have adopted.

If a hospital runs perfectly, that is, without any waste, it can be financially profitable. However, there are numerous occurrences every year in every facility of human error, the primary source of waste in healthcare. Rarely does waste, in the form of a medical error, get attributed to poor or improper training.

So the fact that 5s Lean brings order and organization to the natural chaos of healthcare reduces the incidence of error. Waste and clutter has been proven to lead to human error in healthcare. Reduce waste, reduce clutter, and you reduce the incidence of human error. Correcting or treating the human error creates unplanned costs. These are the costs that create the financial challenges.

The U.S. Department of Health and Human Services reported that in 2008, about 1 in 7 Medicare hospital patients were harmed from medical care. The financial tolls are obvious; if a hospital harms a patient, they must fix that situation. The fix becomes an unplanned expense. And when this happens to 1 in 7 Medicare patients, the rate of error is high and unsustainable for most hospital budgets over the long-term. To make matters even more taxing, Medicare reimbursements have been cut for care associated with hospital acquired conditions.

So the correlation between medical errors and hospital acquired conditions has a direct impact on healthcare organizations' financial results. A successful 5s Lean Healthcare culture, one where everyone on staff buys in to the need to continuously sort, set in order, shine, standardize, and sustain, will clearly reduce the clutter and un-cleanliness that causes human error in healthcare.

As a result, not only do fewer medical errors or healthcare acquired conditions arise that strain the operational budget, quality of care improves (by definition of there being fewer errors), and patient safety increases in proportion as well.

Chapter 6: Starting 5s Lean in Your Healthcare Organization

Waste and clutter: Experts working within healthcare have long observed that these two villains cause human error and financial harm.

Like most dire problems, they are interwoven through a large network of issues and processes. As a result, they affect top priorities such as medical outcomes, patient care quality and safety, and the financial challenge of improving all of those quality indicators at a lower cost.

Healthcare leaders have been adopting techniques that have proven successful in the manufacturing industry on a large scale since the early 1990's. 5s Lean has helped manufacturers, and now healthcare organizations, streamline operations and management, and reduce waste and clutter.

5s is more than a process or system. To really make it work, it has to be adopted by staff in all departments as a culture or mindset. It is on-going, and everyone must participate. Sounds like a lot of work, but when it works, it can dramatically affect all of those deeply interwoven issues that have a huge impact on a healthcare organization, such as:

- Reduced Waste (time, supplies, re-admissions, medical error corrections).
- Reduced Clutter.

- Improved Patient Satisfaction Scores (cleaner, quieter facilities rate higher).
- Improved Medical Outcomes.
- Improved Financial Outcomes (improved utilization of resources, greatly reduced waste of supplies)

To have this much impact on such a wide variety of parameters, healthcare leaders have some important planning to do before the 5s process can be launched.

Step 1: Establish a 5s Leadership Team

This should be no great mystery to healthcare organizations. Hospitals routinely put together leadership teams, sometimes called "sponsorship teams" or "project teams" when they undergo a major capital building project.

The 5s Leadership Team should contain influential leaders who are well-organized from the organization. This team should be the initial experts in 5s knowledge. That doesn't mean they have to be experts when they are chosen to serve on the team. At this stage, they need only see the value 5s can have in helping the organization achieve its stated goals. Once on the team, the members should grow to become the repository for 5s knowledge and expertise and keep the program moving forward.

Step 2: Plant the seeds for a positive mindset to grow

It's no secret that change does not come easy for people. Therefore, it is worth the up-front investment to make sure people understand the value this change will bring to them. Start by training managers and supervisors in the 5s process, and show them the results others in their positions are having. For example, take them on a "field trip" to tour a facility that has already adopted a 5s culture so they can see it in action. The 5s Leadership Team should ask for input on how best to roll out 5s processes to various departments. Collaborate on how best to win the rest of the staff over to become committed to making their facility a better place.

Important Note: Keep the instruction of the 5s process somewhat brief at this point. The goal first is to persuade them of the value of the 5s Lean method.

Step 3: Planning

At this stage, put a plan to paper. Now that the mindset has been established and people have bought into the concept of removing clutter and waste from their workplace, document how the plan should be executed. Spread these plans throughout the facility so that they are readily accessible to anyone needing them for guidance.

Other key actions during this phase that will help structure your plan:
- Establish a budget.

- Allocate space for 'sorting'.
- Schedule times for performing the 5s steps.

Step 4: Spread the Word

By this stage, leaders at many levels have learned enough about 5s to recognize the value of what is in it for them. Now is the time to give them formal training on 5s methods, and introduce 5s to the entire staff. Successful tactics at this stage include lunch and learn sessions, seminars, and field trips to sites where 5s has already been implemented successfully.

Step 5: Build Staff Participation and Acceptance

Make it easy for staff to collaborate on your 5s process. They will want to tailor this effort so that it fits their unique needs. Let them. Set up ways for staff to offer their ideas and suggestions. This is the real root of 5s Lean. The people who best understand the work are the ones who are actually doing the work every day. Give them the chance to inform leaders how to improve their workflow and storage challenges. If they know what the goals are that the leadership team wants to achieve, then the staff will be full of ideas to help achieve those goals.

Implementation

You are finally there. Empower department leaders and team leaders to begin their own 5s Process:
- Sort
- Set in Order
- Shine

- Standardize
- Sustain

The 5s Leadership Team should continue to meet to monitor progress. Remember to share the results with the entire staff so that they can see how the changes they have made are helping the organization achieve its goals of better healthcare at a lower cost.

Chapter 7: Implementing 5s Lean in Your Healthcare Organization

A lot of preparation and planning goes into launching a 5s Lean methodology in a healthcare organization. Leaders, supervisors, and staff all have to be sold on the value a 5s process will bring to their work. Some people will listen to the argument for 5s, and its promise to reduce clutter and waste, and how it impacts healthcare quality, patient safety and satisfaction, and financial performance, but then ask, "Ok. But what does that look like?"

Hospitals store millions of dollars of surgical supplies every day. Often, the storage system includes some portion of those supplies in the Central Sterile Supply Storage, and a smaller portion stored in the operating room core.

A primary goal for improving healthcare efficiency today is point-of-need storage. Point-of-need is often used interchangeably with point-of-care. The idea is to have the supplies located close to where the work is performed so that staff spends less time hunting for and gathering what they need. Therefore, hospitals are trying to find efficient ways to have as many supplies at the patient's bedside or in the operating room core as possible. The operating room core is located closer to the patients and surgical team than a hospital's central sterile supply room.

For the last several decades, the de facto solution has been stationary wire racks. Rows and rows of wire rack shelving are labelled in an attempt to keep things organized, and supplies are stacked on top of each other.

Hospital materials managers are now looking outside their industry for a better solution.

High-density mobile storage is not new. It has been used for decades in other workplace environments, such as office space to store files, libraries to hold books, museums to store works of art while not on display, and in doctor's offices to store patient charts.

But now materials managers have learned that these units can be put to good use in the central sterile supply rooms, and even closer to the point-of-care, in the operating room core.

The shelving units sit on wheeled carriages that travel on rails. People move them either manually, mechanically assisted, or by powered key pad.

Healthcare Supply Managers have removed the rows of inefficient wire racks, and have replaced them with far fewer high-density mobile storage systems. These systems are designed to at least double the storage capacity of static shelving.

Recognized Benefits
- Reduced travel time for staff. Supplies are close at hand in the operating room core.
- Reduced waiting.

- Adjustable shelving and bins to accommodate changing sizes of supply packages.
- Less unused space, both on the shelves and in between aisles.
- Better organized system for small unit supplies by using various sized drawers, bins, and shelves.
- The mobile systems enable managers to specify clear, see-through end panels and doors so that staff can get a quick visual on items for better inventory control and location identification.
- These same glass or flexi-glass doors help keep items protected from dust.
- Shelves can be slanted for gravity-fed dispensing. This is especially handy for items like sutures that have an expiration date. Wasted supplies due to expiration will be reduced drastically, saving critical budget.

Ideas for Items to Store in the Operating Room Core's High-Density Mobile System
- Sterile supplies for surgery
- Sterile cases and procedure kits for surgery
- Sterile instruments for surgery
- Replacement parts for orthopaedic surgical procedures
- Specialized supplies needed for cardiac surgical operating rooms and neurosurgery operating rooms
- Soft goods
- Syringes

- Catheters
- Sutures
- Stents
- Dressings.

Chapter 8: Why 5s Lean Matters and How It's Done

A laboratory is a target-rich environment for process improvement because it is a room full of processes. Where there is process, there is waste. So the 5s Lean mindset can be so beneficial when lab staff adopt it as standard operating procedure for how they work. 5s Lean methods help people identify wasted time and wasted materials in their work process. When the staff makes small, incremental changes to reduce these types of waste, productivity increases and the process in question becomes more profitable.

Lean methods of waste reduction have proven successful in manufacturing plants for decades. This bodes well for healthcare laboratories because they are set up to operate very similarly to a manufacturing plant. In a lab, raw materials in the form of a blood sample or some other type of bodily specimen (human tissue, or a tumour for example) are the "input" for the process.

The sample moves from one person to another in a series of steps within the lab in order to turn this raw material into something else. In manufacturing, that end result is a "finished good" of some kind, i.e. a car, a plane, a chair, even food. In a healthcare lab, the finished good, or the "product" that the lab produces is often a diagnosis or a lab test result that allows the doctor to make a diagnosis for a patient.

Example: A tumour enters the lab process as a raw material. It flows through a multi-step process for testing and analysis. At the end of the process, it may be declared "cancerous". The doctor is then able to take this "product" or "finished-good" (the test result) and make a diagnosis that her patient has some type of cancer.

The testing and analysis is expensive to perform. There are human labour costs, supplies, and equipment involved, as well as electricity, and building costs, to name just a few. Therefore, it becomes very important to strive toward having no wasted time or materials in the process design itself. Here are some ideas about how to achieve this design.

Sort and Set in Order

Make sure everything has its proper place and a visual indicator, both on a macro-level and on a micro-level. At the macro-level, sort and set each bench so that it is placed on the lab floor plan in a way that makes sense to reduce waste. For example, some questions to ask would be:
1. Are the benches that perform the work at the beginning of a given process closest to where the raw material is brought into the lab?
2. Are the benches that perform the most frequent work easily accessible?
3. Are the benches that perform less frequent work located so that they are not in the way of high-traffic patterns to and from the busier benches?

4. Are visual dividers low enough so that teammates can see each other?

This often helps with transition steps from within a bench as well as hand-offs to another bench for the following step in the process.

1. Have you taken advantage of putting as many benches, tables, carts, and equipment on casters so that they can be mobile?
Giving lab staff the power and control to flexibly relocate these items as needed allows them to make the small, incremental improvements that are the hallmark of Lean.

2. Are there any other visual inhibitors that can be removed?
This will also help improve interaction between staff and create better workflow. At the micro-level, contained within the lab bench itself, there are also ways to sort materials and equipment and set them in order to improve workflow.

3. At the bench top, have you sorted supplies so that the frequently-used items are separate and more accessible than the less frequently-used items?

4. Have you taken advantage of the many ingenious storage supplies available to help you keep your materials in order, clean, and accessible?

There are many kinds of clear acrylic dispensers that enable lab staff to easily locate each supply, as well as alert them when inventory runs low and needs to be refilled.

5. Have you clearly labelled your bench-top supplies so that they are easy to find?
This will provide easy visual identification.

6. Have you labelled your bench-top supplies in an easily understood format, and standardized it to follow the rest of the lab's protocol?
This will help keep workflow humming when a staff member is replaced due to being off sick, on vacation, or leaving altogether and is replaced by a new staff.

Use these questions to guide you through your space-planning and design. They will lead you to a work flow that will be sure to produce a return on your 5s Lean investment.

Chapter 9: Turn Your Waiting Room Into a 5s Lean Showcase

The efficiency and cleanliness of the registration area of an hospital, residential home or Doctors Surgery makes a vital first impression on patients and family members. One cannot dismiss the importance of this impression, because of the growing competition among healthcare providers to attract new patients, as well as the patient satisfaction surveys that are becoming increasingly tied to insurance reimbursements in the US and Government funding in the UK.

If you are convinced of the worthwhile return on investment that the 5s Lean mindset and culture will have on your healthcare organization, you have done the initial planning, and are now ready to roll it out in a tangible way, here are some ideas for your patient registration area.

1. Signs, Way-Finding, and Messaging

One of the first things people will notice when they enter a medical facility of any type, whether it be a hospital or a clinic, will be the signs mounted on walls or stand-alone displays. This is where a healthcare organization can set the tone for efficiency and competence.

Some signs provide rules and instructions, other help people find their way around your facility. This demonstrates to people that you have sorted out your workspace and have organized where the different types of work your clinic performs will happen. You have set your clinic in order and have welcomed guests into your space with directions that are easy to find and easy to follow.

Shine by keeping your signs clean and organized by mounting them in an attractive way with a messaging board for example, or even by using a digital kiosk or monitor.

2. Patient Education and Entertainment

Brochure and magazine holders are great tools to sort, set in order, shine, standardize, and sustain your patient education literature as well as consumer magazines that entertain people while they wait for the next step in your healthcare process.

By giving everything its place, your guests will tend to follow your lead and comply with your 5s Lean method, perhaps without even realizing they are doing it!

3. Hygiene Stations

Another key component for building a great first impression is the infection prevention station. These are typically found to be stand-alone units on the floor, wall-mounted, or countertop mounted. If you are shopping around for these, try search terms like "hand hygiene station", "infection prevention station", and "respiratory hygiene station".

There are many benefits and a variety of different products that are suitable for hand hygiene. These hygiene kits or stations are best placed at the points of entry into the building, into the clinic registration area, and into the examination area. During flu season, respiratory hygiene becomes very important too. In these hygiene or infection prevention stations, you will typically find a hand sanitizer gel, tissues, and face masks. They are not just used by surgical teams in the operating rooms anymore.

4. Document Management to Standardize and Sustain

A successful 5s Lean healthcare culture has staff members that follow and sustain standards. In the 1990's, this led to shelves and countertops filled with three-ring binders. This is an unattractive and overwhelming sight, not only to the patients but also the staff. There are silver ion-treated (germ-killing) desktop document display holders that look much more professional. When guests step up to the registration and check-in desk, they are impressed by a registration specialist who has all of their information at their fingertips. Condensing the volumes of binders down to "one-sheet" policies and procedures will make your organization's standards more accessible and easier to follow. Both of which contribute to better compliance.

Chapter 10: 5s Lean Help You Stay Profitable

Many phlebotomy labs are characterized by tight space, lots of supplies densely packed in that space, and a steady stream of staff and patients flowing in and out of the room. Blood draw areas are often procedurally driven, so swift turn-around is critical for a productive and profitable clinic.

By applying the 5s Lean methodology (Sort, Set in Order, Shine, Standardize, and Sustain) phlebotomy leaders can reduce wasted steps. This saves time on process and permits more time for quality. Here are ways to help realize that goal.

1. Sort

Start with sorting supplies in your phlebotomy area. Separate the frequently used from the infrequently used. Separate the important from the unnecessary. Designate space for sorting. Do it quickly.

These are the basic, straight-forward instructions to get started. Once items have been sorted accordingly, look for storage containers whether it be shelving, bins, or drawers that will enable you to move on to the next step.

2. Set in Order

Now take the medical supplies you have sorted and set them into shelves, lockers, carts, bins, and drawers that make sense for your workspace. Less frequently used and unimportant items should be stored further away while the more important, frequently used supplies should have top priority in your most accessible storage spaces.

Every item should have its own location, and labelled clearly so that staff can find them in a hurry. The labelling system you use, and the way you set the supplies in order, (literally how you position the items in the drawer or on the shelf for example), should be easy to understand for a new staff member with minimal training, and it should reduce the chance for human error to allow someone to mistakenly grab the incorrect item.

3. Shine

Establishing a high standard for keeping the phlebotomy area clean is essential for infection prevention, efficiency, and safety. Simply by maintaining an organized work area, you have started the Shine process. Like the other "S"'s in 5s, this process is never complete. All of them are ongoing for the staff. That is why 5s Lean should be thought of as a "mindset" rather than a "program".

Another important aspect of "Shine" however is keeping the phlebotomy work and storage areas clean. There are various disinfectant wipes that are sold in accessible and convenient tubs that can be mounted to the wall or set on a countertop. Keep them handy. These antimicrobial wipes should be part of the daily workflow, every day. Wipe down chairs, countertops, and other surfaces. Choose phlebotomy carts that have plastic drawers so that they can be wiped down over the long-term without getting rusty. I like to choose carts and drawers that have rounded corners on the outside for staff safety, and rounded corners on the inside of drawers so that dirt and germs can be wiped out by staff. The right angle corners make it too easy for dirt and bacteria to build up and hide from cleaners.

4. Standardize

One way to standardize the methodology and ensure it happens every day is to use supplies that make the rules and the process steps visible.

5. Sustain

If you have done a good job with setting your standards, and getting your phlebotomy staff to buy into the fact that these daily routine tasks of sort, set in order, and shine are habitual, then you are on the right path to lead them toward sustaining the mindset. Like the other steps above, this is a continuous process. The proper mindset is to constantly be on the lookout for supplies to sort and separate, for areas to clean, and for ways to make new small improvements to your work processes. Then implement these incremental process improvements as the new standard to sustain. Until you improve again.

Chapter 11: 5s Lean Culture and Wheelchair Inventory Control

Hospitals are filled with many types of wheelchairs to accommodate the variety of people who need them. Typically, wheelchairs are provided as loaners for internal transport through the facility. But unfortunately, wheelchairs end up becoming lost, or are put into the patient's car when they leave to go home. In other cases, wheelchairs simply never find their way back to where they came from within the facility. They start in one area and revert back to a new, often the closest, storage space once they are no longer needed.

The wheelchair inventory control problem is so common, so pervasive, that it is often accepted as the way it has to be. It doesn't. Developing a 5s Lean culture using the simple methodology can put you back in control of your wheelchair inventory. As a result, you will replace wheelchairs less often, which is expensive, and your staff will waste less time searching for a wheelchair when they need one.

Sort

The 5s Lean method never ends. It is a continuous loop of activity. This is why it is more accurate to think of 5s as a "mindset" or "culture" rather than a "program". You will know your team has adopted this culture when they routinely perform the activities in the method, and especially when they quickly notice when something is out of place and they get it back in order.

Sorting different types of wheelchairs is important so that staff can quickly find the wheelchair they need for the particular patient they want to accommodate. So the foundation step is to sort the most frequently used wheelchairs from the less frequently used. Sort your paediatric wheelchairs, your bariatric wheelchairs, and your adult wheelchairs, and so on.

Set in Order

Next, set the wheelchair types in order. Give them a "home" by storing them in an accessible, clean, organized area. Label the areas as well as the chairs themselves. This will save staff time searching for them and when returning them after they are used.

Some ideas for effective labelling can include:
1. Colour-code your wheelchairs in some way (tags, labels, colour of vinyl, etc.) so that everyone knows where the chair belongs immediately when it is found to be out of its place.
2. Label the storage zone itself so that when returning a paediatric chair there is a clearly designated space for it, and it won't mistakenly get mixed in with the adult chairs for example.

Shine

A 5s Lean mindset will have staff members voluntarily making sure wheelchairs are clean, and the place where they are stored is clean, organized and accessible.

Standardize

Standardize your organizational process by using visual cues, throughout your facility. This will make it easier for staff to quickly adopt the procedure because they will see it everywhere and if they transfer from one department to another the visual cues will be consistent, thus allowing them to maintain the standards. Sort, Set In order, and Shine will then become easy to follow habits that further strengthen your 5s Lean success.

Sustain

Each of these habits roll into one another. They overlap, and must, in order to work. One of the best things you can do to enable the staff to sustain the 5s Lean habits is to make them easy and obvious. They will not be effective unless Sort, Set In Order, Shine, and Standardize become ingrained in the organization's culture.

Chapter 12: Disciplined Daily Management System

Visuals are such an important part of Lean Healthcare, and everyday life for that matter, that it is not surprising that most people focus on the Daily Management Board component of their Daily Management System. After all, it is a visible part of the system, right. This notion can be a bit misleading and can cause employees to miss the true power of the system, akin to ignoring the submerged portion of an iceberg. A true, disciplined Daily Management System should be the nucleus of a sustaining, engaging Lean transformation process. It is not about the boards!

Here is a high-level framework. In addition to the "tip of the iceberg," is your Daily Management System composed of these pieces?

Daily: It is absolutely crucial that everyone in the organization meet daily for 15 to 30 minutes to discuss how they did against yesterday's goals, what they need to accomplish today to satisfy customer demand, and what problems they need to solve to meet their goals. While work and outcomes occur in minutes and hours (and sometimes seconds), we in healthcare are conditioned to look at monthly and quarterly metrics. By then, it is too late to adjust processes to positively impact those metrics. Both outcome and process metrics must be reviewed and acted upon by management daily.

Management: Managers organize and lead teams to achieve the organization's goals in support of its mission. A brief huddle at the beginning of each day with the management team sets the tone for the day by keeping everyone focused on the team's objectives and giving them frequent feedback on their performance. The longer it takes to provide feedback, the less valuable it is.

System: A system is an organized set of processes which delivers value to customers. It is interesting that the customers of the Daily Management System are the managers and team members. The ultimate beneficiaries, however, are the patients. The processes in a Daily Management System include updating the boards each day before the meeting, the meeting itself, and completing the action items that come out of each meeting.

The Daily Management Boards are a powerful visual tool to make the Daily Management System efficient. The boards are not the system. They allow each team and individual to see how they are doing at a glance, which allows them more time to use their teamwork and problem-solving skills. I believe that healthy Daily Management Systems are the single most important ingredient to sustaining a Lean culture in your healthcare organization.

Chapter 13: Waste Reduction

We are big sports fans in our house. When we are watching a sporting event in person, we always like to have a good view of the scoreboard. In fact, if you watch people walk into a stadium, the scoreboard is one of the first places most people look. It is important to know if our favourite team is winning or losing.

How about in your hospital or clinic? What is your scoreboard telling you? One of my favourite questions to ask organizations new to Lean Healthcare is, "How do you know if you are winning or losing? How does frontline staff know they are succeeding?" I often get the response, "As long as no one dies, it's a good day." Have we really set the bar that low?!

As we begin to implement Lean Healthcare principles in an organization, we utilize visual controls in order to help drive continuous improvement and prioritize problem solving activities.

There are two common pitfalls that leaders can make when using a system of visual controls:

1. **No leadership support:** Leaders have to check the scoreboard; they must make it a part of their everyday work to get out to the areas in which they oversee. This will allow them to review the data boards and the associated problem solving by their staff. A

leader's job is to coach and remove roadblocks the teams are having in their problem solving efforts.

2. **Requiring all visual controls to look the same:** Often times leaders latch on to the principle in Lean Healthcare of standardization. However, requiring that all visual boards in the organization "look" the same shows a lack of understanding of the reason behind the visual controls. Allowing areas to own their own data boards and with the History, Pareto, and Problem Solving components should be the standard. The information that gets tracked and subsequently improved can be left up to each functional area of the organization. This typically allows for more creativity and better problem solving.

Accountability is one of those words many people in healthcare throw around. We all want it for ourselves and we especially want our employees to have it. Few leaders know how to get it or how to give it.

Accountability is a willingness to invest in decision-making and express ownership in those decisions. As such, accountability is a core component of Shared Governance.

You may be asking yourself, "Who cares, isn't this book about 5s Lean Healthcare?"

Exactly! A mature lean healthcare organization is based on respect for people. This concept includes moving decision-making to the highest level of expertise, which often is the lowest level of authority or title. Systems and structures are necessary to support good decision making.

Below is a simple example that demonstrates these principles:

Our local hospital is an 80-bed community-based hospital which began implementing lean healthcare principles two-and-a-half years ago. As part of their journey they have placed a heavy emphasis on A3 Problem Solving and have trained approximately 25 percent of their staff in this Lean Healthcare tool. Recent training on lean management systems allowed charge nurses on a med-surgery unit to apply their knowledge of Visual Management and A3 Problem Solving.

In developing their unit's Visual Management, charge nurses were coached to align key areas of focus for the unit with overall organizational goals. As with every patient care unit, expenses were of course among the top three focus areas. Data for labour and non-labour expenses was provided to the charge nurses from the Director and was displayed on a bulletin board in the staff lounge.

This prompted conversations with staff on how the non-labour expenses could be decreased. One observed issue was the disposal of non-used patient hygiene items at discharge. By analyzing this issue, they realized nursing staff routinely brought these items to a room when a patient was admitted, whether or not a patient wanted or needed them. The staff also knew that a second area of focus was patient satisfaction, especially improving scores around involving patients and families in decisions regarding their care.

After discussing the issue with Unit Healthcare Assistants a plan was developed to start the morning shift by rounding on patients, introducing themselves, and providing the patient with a list of hygiene items they might want. Patients checked the items needed and those items were brought to the room. Initial tests of this process included feedback from patients and staff which was overwhelmingly positive. Unit Healthcare Assistants were thrilled that someone finally asked them what they could do to decrease expenses.

While the final data is being counted in terms of the impact this made on unit expenses and patient satisfaction, the charge nurses used a simple method of measurement by collecting the wash basins that were disposed of at discharge. The before and after pictures of the wash basins were posted on the same unit bulletin board.

Imagine if 25 percent of your staff were accountable to implement small solutions to decrease expenses what could happen in your organization?

Chapter 14: Status at a Glance

"Status at a glance" You have no doubt heard the term many times when discussing visual management and the fundamentals of Lean Healthcare. What does it really mean, and how do we ensure that the tools we are implementing truly are telling the story our picture intends?

Manufacturing has focused on visual management for a long time, but how does it apply in Lean Healthcare? The key objectives of visual management are:

- Give the status (Indicator Lights)
- Direct and locate things (Road signs)
- Indicate actions (Traffic Lights)
- Show what is right or wrong (Lines in parking lots)

Although each tool has a different objective, the goal of all visual management tools is the same; "Status at a Glance". For a leader, especially a leader in an organization that is on the pathway to a Lean transformation, visual management is one of the most fundamental and necessary elements to success. The Gemba is focused on coaching and reinforcing the behaviours of our employees that support our departmental objectives which are driven by our strategic initiatives. The Gemba is about observation and our observation is greatly enhanced by the ability to see the "status at a glance."

I was recently in a hospital in the United Kingdom that is in the early stages of a Lean Healthcare transformation. One of the lean facilitators for the institution stopped at a visual management board in a hallway to explain what the board was telling the hospital leadership and employees. The important thing was that he didn't need to explain the board. I was able to look at the board and at a glance know where the questions should be directed. The status of the metrics was easily observable by the simple colour coding of the days of the month to indicate whether the goals were achieved. The board clearly specified good versus bad on a daily basis by the criteria for red and green. I was also impressed that a staff member who was passing by was able to articulate the function of the board as well the meaning for the employees. This was a visual management tool that was doing a very credible job of "status at a glance."

A visual management system in a Lean Healthcare organization is critical to success. The manner in which data and status are presented and communicated is called a visual management board. This powerful tool is designed to fulfil the following fundamentals:

- It should give the status of the process.
- It should direct the leadership to areas that need support.
- It should indicate the actions or countermeasures that are in process.
- It should show normal versus the abnormal, or what is right and what is wrong.

When creating a visual management board, a simple four by four matrix is a good place to begin. The columns reflect the key indicators of the value diamond of a Lean Healthcare organization. Satisfaction, Quality/Safety, Cost and Time. The first row reflects the "History" a run chart of a key indicator for the unit. The second row is "Pareto" what has been determined to be the primary influences or root causes of the failure to meet the goal. The third row is "Problem Solving" typically an A3 depicting the cause or causes that the unit is working on. The fourth and bottom row is the leading indicator data depicting the countermeasure from the A3.

When assessing a visual management board, the criteria are:
- Evidence of visual management practices.
- Evidence that the information within the tools is maintained and current.
- Measurements include goals/targets (expected) and actual results.
- Reasons for "misses" are documented and are driving continuous improvement efforts.
- Evidence of a system of standards and responses.
- Modifications and updates as conditions change.

A colleague of mine has an example that explains this very well:

A unit in a hospital was struggling with discharges. The goal was 80% discharges by 10AM. The run chart showed they were averaging only 40%. Pareto analysis showed the number one cause was patients not ready to be discharged at 10AM. When an A3 was worked through to give more detail it was defined that patients didn't know they were leaving that day and time and they didn't have transportation arranged, among other obstacles. The countermeasure the team decided on was to utilize the whiteboards in the patient rooms to update daily with the prospective discharge date and time for the patient and the patient's family. This countermeasure's data was gathered by the charge nurse in normal rounding and entered directly to a chart on the visual management board (percentage of boards updated that day).

This now provided a leading indicator that could be tested against the overall defect of the failure for timely discharges. In fact, this countermeasure was very successful and subsequently the overall metric did show dramatic improvement.

"Every Picture Tells a Story". We need our pictures to tell the story intended, in a simple focused manner that our employees can easily understand and, just as importantly, be a driving force for the problem solving that is integral to continuous improvement and Lean Healthcare transformations.

Chapter 15: Tracking the Right Metrics

One tool that is often missing is meaningful performance data. Imagine if you were a player on a football team in a league where the score was kept but not known to either team (including the coaches) until the end of the season.

In the same way, as Lean Healthcare leaders, if we don't know how our teams are performing, we can't provide meaningful and effective correction and support. It is true that we have a lot of data in our hospitals and clinics, but the assembly of that data into meaningful form often does not happen or happens way too late. Even then, we as leaders often choose to focus on the wrong things.

Here are a few common pitfalls I see as hospital leadership struggles to put the necessary "scoreboard" in place:

1. Defining objectives or performance metrics at the wrong level. I recently observed a pharmacy team metrics board that showed their goal to be Patient Satisfaction (at the hospital level). This is not a good "scoreboard" for the pharmacy because this team can't own this metric. After some discussion, they agreed that they could rally around a metric that they can control or influence, such as first dose turnaround time.

2. Stale or expired data. I recently learned of a hospital where meaningful Core Measures performance data was not available until up to 180 days after the patient was discharged. There was no way to implement effective performance improvement efforts with data this old.

   The lag in data also made it impossible to determine if process improvements were effective. In cases like this, more timely proxy measures can be effective. Sometimes we have to be willing to consider less than 100 percent precision on a metric in order to get more timely feedback. This will empower the team to understand how they were performing and make adjustments.

3. Too much effort required to update the scoreboard. Making the data difficult to get is a sure way to make certain that it is not compiled and reviewed at the lower levels. It is common to see mid-level managers spend hours per week collecting and collating data from disparate information systems to generate a report. As an alternative, find proxies for these metrics or automate some of the analysis.

4. Over complication of the metric on scoreboards. The trend seems to be that leaders want complicated spreadsheets with detailed analysis for metrics. This leads to a disconnect with the people who do the work.

As an alternative, consider a Visual Management board on the unit that gets updated with each day's performance, forming a trend over time. This will allow the teams better access to their performance and empower the leaders to meet at the board and review the data.

Chapter 16: Red Tag Process in Lean Healthcare

While participating in a recent Workplace Organization event, I was reminded of how the red tag process in Lean Healthcare can suddenly become an issue.

During the sorting step of 5s unnecessary items are removed from a work area. Because teams are often created ad hoc, there is the potential for someone to inadvertently remove an item that is actually needed in providing a service or in patient care. The Lean Healthcare red tag process helps eliminate sorting errors.

The red tag process follows this basic flow:
1. A person identifies an item in question.
2. The person fills out a red tag and attaches it to the item.
3. The person waits for input on the action of red tagging the item.
4. If another person questions the red tag, the people or decision makers for the area determine whether to keep the item or not.
5. If the item is to be kept, the red tag is removed.
6. If the item is not to be kept, it is disposed of, often to a red tag area. This is basically a holding area for items with value but no homes. An item that is not needed in one area may still be put into use in another area. Some

organizations require approval to remove a red tagged item.
7. Items in the red tag area that are not claimed by a designated date should be removed to prevent the area from turning into a dump ground. The disposal can range from selling the equipment, to giving it/auctioning it to employees, to scrapping it.

The red tag system is a safety net that keeps overly eager improvement teams from taking necessary equipment from an area. This is usually one of the main culprits in creating the confusion. A big issue is when an item is only used intermittently, and can look like they are not needed for the service or in the patient care process.

If an item is red tagged and the tag is removed, the item should not just be left as it is. It should have a location designated, and the item itself should be labelled regarding its use. This will keep future teams from red tagging the equipment over and over.

Chapter 17: Airport Analogy as a Great Example of Simplicity

As a road warrior, I spend a lot of time in airports, which makes it easy for me to draw an analogy from the excellent visual control systems in airports.

- The signage leading into the airport allows travellers to know at-a-glance where to park, either to long term, short term or rental car areas.
- From there you are directed to the ticketing and baggage check-in counters and on through security.
- Electronics signs direct you to your gate and the gate attendant directs you through the process of getting on the plane.
- As you exit the plane, there are signs to direct you to the baggage claim area along with directions to access ground travel and additional signage to leave the airport.

From the time I arrive at one airport to the time I leave another, there is an invisible hand guiding me to where I need to go and what I need to do. As you begin your lean healthcare journey, hospitals should begin with an organized approach using these tools. Use the airport analogy as a great example of simplicity!

For consistency, one owner should be managing this process and have a vision of the ideal state for the entire facility (this process goes far beyond just hospital directional signage; the folks that designed the hospital likely didn't get down to the minutiae required by a robust visual management system). It must also be applied to back-of-house areas as well; such as office areas and storage rooms.

The staff will understand the benefits after the first couple of 5s events and a snowball effect will occur to quickly implement throughout the facility. The approach of teaching a smaller group of leaders about 5s and implementing just through them does not usually sustain itself. They can easily lose sight of the overall vision.

I have observed the most success when there is a train-the-trainer program in place, with all trainers teaching the visual management system, and the sustainment plan is managed with audits, goals and Gemba walks (coaching) by the leadership.

Chapter 18: Eliminating Some of the Built in Waste

Too often I lead teams whose goal it is to improve the workflow of caregivers, only to find that the team is hamstrung by a facility design that doesn't support that team's vision. There are all kinds of explanations for how these physical design barriers come to be, but I won't try to list them all. I would rather focus on one of these explanations and leave the other hundred or so.

The focus of Lean healthcare is waste elimination. It is also widely accepted that two of the most prevalent forms of waste in healthcare are motion and transportation. A common cause of both these types of waste is searching for supplies and equipment. It is my experience that the way we design our facilities creates an environment where we are destined to have significant searching. Many well meaning healthcare designers have actually exacerbated this searching by using typical design paradigms regarding the use of casework and cabinetry.

Let me explain:

In healthcare design, there is a tendency to furnish most workspaces with plenty of cabinetry and casework. Often, there seems to be a "more is better" approach and designers endeavour to squeeze as many cabinets and drawers as possible into a given space. I want to challenge this approach. The number and size of cabinets and drawers in a work space should be defined by the work flow in that space. Sometimes this means that we will have fewer cabinets and drawers than the space will accommodate. I realize that this is a counter-intuitive assertion. I know because from care givers I hear, "we never have enough cabinets to store all our stuff." And from designers I hear, "in the interest of the staff, I look for opportunities to maximize the use of casework so that there will be plenty of storage."

Let me also clarify that for purposes of this chapter, I am referring to clinical care areas rather than public spaces or even areas where patients will spend a lot of time.

Certainly, cabinetry serves a useful purpose. It serves to hold the stuff that we wish to store near the point of use. It can also provide a level of security and safety for our stuff and our patients. Cabinetry also provides an aesthetical benefit by obscuring the negative appearance of clinical supplies. But, in these clinical areas, where patients rarely go, safety, security and appearance are secondary or tertiary considerations. The primary consideration instead, is quick and efficient access to care supplies for purposes of restocking and providing care. In this case, more visibility to the supplies rather than less visibility is desirable. Cabinetry and casework are tools that limit visibility. The result is more searching and an unnecessary barrier to ensuring reliable replenishment.

The design of casework and cabinetry should be purposeful. There are certainly appropriate applications of casework and cabinetry but, its use should not be the default in all situations. It is the front-line staff, with their intimate knowledge of the workflows in a workspace who should inform the placement of design elements. Favouring more open, visible storage will provide for a more efficient workflow by easing access to the supplies and increasing the likelihood of proper replenishment.

Given that I have no architectural or design expertise, how can I recommend a new paradigm in healthcare design? It is the front-line staff that I have worked with that have, through observation of their waste-filled current state processes, pointed out this built-in waste. They have, on several occasions, recommended a more open and visible storage in work spaces such as Medication Rooms, Nourishment areas, procedure rooms and the like. But, by the time these counter-measures are requested, it is too late. The prospect of replacing cabinetry valued at several thousand dollars is a non-starter with most leaders. So, they continue to deal with an inefficient process and develop other workarounds.

What is the solution? Engage front-line staff earlier in the design phases of a hospital construction or remodel project. By doing so, we can eliminate some of this built in waste. This is just one example but there are many potential benefits that can be realized by applying Lean Healthcare principles during the design of a healthcare facility.

Chapter 19: Leadership in a Lean Healthcare Environment

In one of my books; "Lean Healthcare", I proposed that an institution involved in a Lean Healthcare journey that limits its focus to Kaizen Events, runs the risk of finding itself in an organization characterized by "pockets" of success. These pockets of success can only exist temporarily. Similar to the bubbles in a champagne glass they emerge; rise to the fore-front as shining examples of what is achievable and eventually burst as conditions change. I further proposed that to move beyond Kaizen Events means asking three key questions:
1. How do we accelerate the accomplishment of our business strategy?
2. How do we lead in a Lean Healthcare environment?
3. How do we proactively manage change and align our systems and structures to support what we are trying to achieve?

Most of the feedback I received on this thought-piece was inquiries into Question 2. We know we need to lead differently in a Lean environment, but how do we get there from here?

Strong and active coaching is central to Lean leadership. Coaching moves beyond just the results and into the methods. This is often an alien concept. In a management by objective organization, if a bad process yields a good result, it is a good thing. In a

Lean environment, if a bad process yields a good outcome, it is not a good thing. The team either got very lucky or worked very hard to overcome a bad process. Neither is desired. You often hear Senior Leadership "buy-in" cited as a primary cause of failed transformation efforts. Personally, I believe that we more frequently fail to adequately prepare front-line leadership and mid-level managers to become effective coaches and resource allocators. I believe that this is perhaps the most profound leverage point in creating a leadership advantage and in sustaining transformations.

In a Lean environment the ability to see waste and eliminate it from processes must become a coached, nurtured, and highly developed skill-set within the front-line employee. In many organizations, front-line and mid-level leaders find success and growth through the ability to work through (but more frequently around) problems. This limits the spread of a critical skill-set within the front-line as these leaders either continue to drive the work-around activity through daily fire-fighting, attempt to solve problems from outside of the gemba, or are just too busy to coach. To start enabling a coaching environment and facilitate the development of strong front-line and mid-level leaders, there are three key competencies to focus on.

1. The ability to both define and operationalize leadership standard work.
2. The ability to both design and implement visual management systems and visual controls.

3. The ability to solve problems to the root cause.

Are there others? Of course, however, focusing on these three will provide leverage by "pulling" the majority of other skills along.

Leadership standard work has been described as the "highest leverage tool in the Lean management system." It is based on the idea that all work (including that of supervisors, managers and executives) should be "specified for content, sequence, timing, location and outcome." What makes this tool exceptionally effective is that, when well defined and operationalized, it drives process definition, disciplined adherence to process and daily accountability. It sets the standard and helps the front line recognize problems. More importantly it compels action and drives coaching efforts.

Visual controls and visual management systems also help the team to recognize problems and until they are recognized as problems they remain unsolved. They also, more importantly, prompt action. This aids in setting the expectation that problems are solved, as surfaced, within the current stream of work. When visual management and leadership standard work are well designed and implemented, they have the ability to create within the front line a strong linkage between strategic imperatives and specific behaviours. The reinforcement of these specific behaviours and the development of requisite skills becomes the basis of coaching.

Finally, in order for front-line employees to get comfortable solving problems at a root cause level as surfaced within the work, they need both a simple problem solving methodology and the support of a coach. A3 problem solving provides an approach that is easy to understand and implement. However, without the support of a competent coach, the effectiveness of the tools is marginalized.

Building leadership competency with an emphasis on coaching for both results and methods drives organizational growth and reinforces the linkages between strategy and behaviour, and between action and result. By beginning with front-line and mid-manager capability in the development and deployment of the tools described above, it is possible to gain significant leverage. This leverage enables the pull for other necessary skills that move the organization beyond Kaizen Events and becoming Lean into actually being Lean. Developing leadership moves the organization from pockets of success to a clear and sustainable competitive advantage.

Chapter 20: 5s Reduce Financial Pressure

Nobody could have escaped the intense publicity surrounding the global credit crunch and the difficult financial situation many are facing.

One of the most common tools used in Lean methodology is 5s, and is the foundation for standard work. 5s enables teams to focus on the root cause of waste, establishes standards for basic organization and orderliness that improves work flow.

The 5s's refer to Sort, Set, Shine, Standardize and Sustain.

Frequently during this 5s process we have come across some significant volumes of inventory and some surprising and unusual finds including:
- 500,000 sheets of paper; 4 years supply.
- 3 years supply of envelopes.
- 9 years supply of diagnostics testing medium.
- 9 years supply of bleach.
- 14 months supply of ink cartridges.
- Out of date scalpel blades and reagent.
- 990 tea spoons in a pathology basement!

This is what many refer to as stock; Lean calls this Inventory, where excess and out of date supplies are stored in the workplace. All inventory takes up space, although a frequent complaint from many staff is the lack of space, and of course space costs money too.

More importantly, is the amount of money invested in this "stock", some of which could be out of date before it even used.

Take for example paper for printing reports, which are pre printed with the hospital name and logo, designed for a specific type of matrix printer. When 6 years supply of paper is purchased and a generous discount is given for bulk purchase; it seems like a good deal. When an opportunity arises to replace the old troublesome printer, with a faster more efficient and reliable printer, a four year supply of useless paper is the result.

The storage space required takes up a whole storeroom for this one item, time required to disposition its status and so on. What seemed like a good opportunity has now become a burden and the waste of "excess inventory" and a financial cost pressure.

Frequently systems have been set up because of a single previous failure in the supply chain turning everyone into squirrels and the hording of inventory, which is further compounded by the lack of visual management of the inventory.

If we apply this process to our own weekly domestic purchases to save money in the short term? The next time you go to your local supermarket would your shopping list be:
- 9 years supply of cornflakes.
- 3 years supply of baked beans.
- 500,000 toilet paper rolls.

- 14 months supply of bread.
- 6 months supply of apples.

Can you afford to do this? Do you have the space to store this amount of inventory or the capital to build more storage space? How many of the items will be out of date before you can use it?

Food for Thought.

Whilst the NHS in the UK is prepared to order and store goods in these quantities, suppliers have no need to invest in warehousing facilities given the NHS has become the free warehouse!

Chapter 21: Success Factors for 5s

We took a quick poll today during a training class for Lean facilitators on their common experiences with barriers and struggles in sustaining 5s efforts as part of a Lean healthcare implementation. The top 10 success factors for 5s that we agreed on can be grouped as below:

Purpose for 5s

1. Make a clear link between 5s and the elimination of waste. This may seem obvious, but because it's intuitive for people with shallow understanding of Lean to see the benefit of cleaning for the sake of looking good, 5s can lose its link with improvement through waste elimination. Show how 5s helps eliminate each of the 8 types of waste.

2. Explicitly identify how 5s supports other Lean systems. It is clear that 5s is a fundamental aspect of visual management and making problems and abnormalities (waste) immediately visible. Built in quality also relies heavily on 5s, as does workplace safety. Continuous flow is enabled directly by Total Productive Maintenance (TPM) and Single Minute Exchange of Dies (SMED), which are built on strong 5s discipline.

3. Show how 5s saves. Clients have found various supplies, raw materials, machines, space and other

resources as a result of sorting activity, enabling them to not buy things or invest in assets while these "5s-ed" items are consumed. Because 5s supports waste elimination, direct profits may be hard to attribute to a specific 5s "before and after" example, but this is easier when 5s is part of a kaizen effort to balance workloads and free up people, reduce changeover time and reduce inventory, or open up space and stop paying for storage space.

5s and People

4. Lead by example. Nobody who is teaching 5s should shirk it. If you can't find personal purpose for doing 5s, how can you expect others to find it? Maintain personal 5s for a few months, and then teach through your own personal testimonial of resistance, barriers and struggle to sustain. Don't be that chain-smoking doctor who warns others of the harms of tar intake.

5. Make 5s mandatory. "Should 5s be a requirement?" is a common question. Should safety and quality be mandatory? What about coming to work on time? What about following established work standards? What about the use of foul language in the workplace? To some degree, it is up to each employer and manager to draw this line, and whether or not maintaining excellent 5s is considered a job requirement says a lot about leadership.

6. Motivate and reward excellence in 5s, just as you would reward excellence in any endeavour. There is debate on whether people should pay for kaizen ideas

that come from participation in suggestion programs. Why not pay people to do the "manager's job" of thinking creatively and solving problems? Or do we just want the managers to make the big bucks and solve all of our problems? People should be motivated first through intrinsic (non material or monetary reward) through praise and recognition, and then through extrinsic (tangible) rewards.

The 5s Process

7. Clean as you go. Sorting through that 5-foot tall filing cabinet full of documents from who-knows-when is definitely not on the top of anyone's list. Every time you open the drawer to add or retrieve a file, take something out that is questionable and re-file (set in the right place) red tag or throw it away (sort). This makes 5s relatively easy. Some factories clean up for 15 minutes at the end of the day. How about for 5 minutes, three times per day? How often do hospitals and restaurants clean dirty surfaces?

8. Go see. Audit the 5s using score sheets, and give constructive feedback where 5s scores are low. Ask the "5 why" questions and offer support. Make it easy to do 5s.

9. Spend most of your 5s effort on follow up and continuation. Keep in place the gains you have made, and learn what it takes to do this. It is better to have a rock solid foundation and excellent 5s in one area than to have great 5s all across the factory, which won't sustain for 2 months.

5S for the Planet

10. Yes I have disrespected our life-sustaining ecosystem by purchasing too many post-its and keeping them buried in various parts of my travelling bag of Lean tricks. Multiply this time the actions of dozens of consultants over the years at Gemba and we have an oversupply in our office. We humbly apologize. If every person who over-consumes due to a poorly developed sense of what is enough, or a lack of 5s discipline could just sort, straighten and sustain, we would have a few more trees cleaning our air and housing our birds.

Chapter 22: The Sixth S

Hospitals today face the dilemma of providing continued levels of service quality as well as patient safety and security at lesser costs. Financial challenges have been the top concern of hospital CEOs for the last eight years, according to the American College of Healthcare Executives' (ACHE's) annual survey of issues confronting hospitals.

These challenges, which are as prevalent in other industries as they are in healthcare, necessitate a rethinking of how budgets get balanced and how new ideas can keep operations running smoothly.

This is perhaps why organizational systems such as 5s Lean have gone beyond their origins within the realm of manufacturing and have spread into other industries.

5s Lean has been proven an effective remedy for core complications within disorganized factories. A successful 5s program is designed to assist facilities in reducing wastefulness, found in operations and management. In healthcare, experts have attributed waste and clutter as the cause of human error a secondary ailment plaguing healthcare facilities today.

There is vast information available on programs that fix these problems, however, very few have been adapted specifically for healthcare. A clinical 5s program within healthcare was conceptualized in the mid-1990s and has brought order and prosperity to numerous hospitals over the last decade and a half.

It is now more than ever important that struggling facilities take the necessary steps forward, examining the system and how its implementation can bring positive results.

Safety is the sixth S and it is an integral part of 5s by examining five specific 5s events in acute care facilities. We provide two arguments for how safety is linked to 5s.
1. Safety is affected by 5s events, regardless of whether safety is a specific goal.
2. Safety can and should permeate all five S's as part of a comprehensive plan for system improvement.

Reports of 5s events from five departments in one health system were used to evaluate how changes made at each step of the 5s impacted safety.

Safety was affected positively in each step of the 5s through initial safety goals and side effects of other changes.

The case studies show that 5s can be a mechanism for improving safety. Practitioners may reap additional safety benefits by incorporating safety into 5s events through a safety analysis before the 5s, safety goals and considerations during the 5s, and follow-up safety analysis.

Chapter 23: Conclusion

Lean principles, originally developed for manufacturing, are being applied to the operation and design of healthcare facilities with the goals of eliminating waste, reducing patient waiting time, improving patient safety, and lowering healthcare costs.

There are many differences between the traditional design process and one that incorporates Lean operations improvement activities in the design process, including philosophy, perspective, design milestones, amount of time spent in each phase and the people involved in the design.

Traditional Design Process	Lean Driven Design Process
Design Focus	Focus on processes that add value for the patient, staff and family members
Starts with programming	Starts with observation of operational processes
User groups are made up of staff leaders within a department or service	Value-stream focused teams include key stakeholders who are involved across the whole process of delivering the service to the patient are used to analyze the process
Each user group provides feedback to designers about their departments or services	Multidisciplinary consensus based, future-state processes drive the development of the floor plan
Floor plan diagrams are adjusted to accommodate existing operations and processes	Floor plan diagrams are used to validate the value stream, optimize future improvements

The Traditional Design Process, led by an architecture team, typically follows these phases:

Master Planning: This phase typically begins with a strategic plan analyzing how the facility will renew itself over time. Master plans often focus on architecture rather than operations, creating diagrams, plans and renderings of what the building(s) could look like in the future.

Pre-design: The architectural team explores concepts for site, functional program block diagrams and adjacencies along with budget and time frame with the hospital leadership. As pre-design progresses, the program begins to take shape, describing the number and size of rooms and departments based on historical data, formulas and projected volumes. If operational processes have not been reviewed prior to programming, unnecessary spaces may be added to the program. The team develops a few options for the design and form of the facility based on the programmatically informed block diagrams. Pre-design ends with the leadership selecting a scheme to be further developed in next phases.

Schematic Design: During schematic design, the initial block diagrams begin to evolve into departments with rooms. Adjacencies and circulation patterns are established and building support spaces including elevators, stairs and columns are located. The architectural team meets with user groups that typically include department managers and select staff members to review and refine the plans. Other disciplines are added into the team, such as engineers and landscape designers to further refine various aspects of design. Schematic design ends with sign off on locations of departments, adjacencies and key rooms. The general contractor may be involved in this phase or in design development to study the work for feasibility and cost.

Design Development: This phase focuses on refining each room, exploring placement of equipment, casework, electrical, telecommunications and IT systems. Meetings with user groups occur to discuss the operational flow of individual rooms. At this phase, it can be difficult to change departmental circulation and major component placement.

Bidding/ Documents/ Construction: After the design development, meetings with the user groups end and the team prepares construction documents, finalizing the decisions made in design development. Traditionally, each discipline has an individual contract and coordination has to be managed while maintaining the schedule, which can be difficult.

Move-in/ Post occupancy: Upon completion of the hospital, architects and engineers review operating procedures of specific areas, including the physical plant and HVAC systems (Heating, Ventilation, and Air-Conditioning), with key hospital staff. In some instances, a cohesive plan for move-in is created and followed to better locate supplies and equipment.

Traditional design is, more often than not, begun without an extensive review of the existing operations and processes in the current facility to determine what may be needed to evolve the quality and efficiency of care to meet the demands of an ever changing healthcare market.

Another approach to healthcare facility design, the Lean-Driven Design Process deliberately engages the facility stakeholders in the initial design process, with a focus on reviewing operational processes to eliminate waste and improve efficiency.

This review yields a plan for how the hospital would like to operate that forms the basis for the architectural design.

Master Planning: As in traditional design, master planning begins with the development of a strategic plan that analyzes how the facility will renew itself over time. However, in Lean-Driven Design, the focus is on how the provision of healthcare could be improved in the future. Data is collected for service areas and ideas for how these areas might work together in the future are developed. If the project is located on a green field site, the team can utilize a tool developed by Toyota, 3P, which stands for product (patient care), process and preparation, to evaluate the optimal services and operations for the project. This tool offers the team a way to think about new and improved methods for eliminating waste through product and process design.

Pre-design: In pre-design, hospital leaders continue to develop the 3P. Teams, consisting of the architecture team, operations consultants, staff and hospital leaders, are formed to explore day-to-day operations and determine which service areas will be impacted by the project and to plan, at a high level, how these services could be carried out more efficiently in the future.

Process Mapping: A clear departure from the traditional design approach, Process Mapping takes an in-depth look at existing and future hospital processes. The teams examine each operational process from the point of view of the patient, staff and family members, highlighting value-added activities and non-value-added activities through observation and process mapping of the current state of operations. Each step in a process is mapped diagrammatically with additional layers of analysis, such as the time it takes to complete the task and the value of that task, and then added to the diagram. Once the current state maps for each area are completed, unnecessary steps and problems are discovered and solutions are brainstormed to create future state maps showing how processes will be done more efficiently at the new facility. This phase differs from the traditional design approach in that there is considerable effort in the early phases gathering information, defining value and reviewing processes to inform the program and design effort.

Design: The traditional design process phases, schematic design and design development, are focused on achieving the level of detail and documentation required for design approval and cost estimation of a facility's design. The Lean-driven design process combines these phases to create an integrated approach that relies on the information gathered about intended operations of the service lines discovered in the early phases of the project to support the design effort. The design is focused on efficiency and standardization to limit process variation, increase flexibility and improve the quality of care. This focus strengthens the future operational processes, encourages smaller design iterations, and results in less design rework. Small, simple mock-ups are created to allow teams to run quick process simulations and test design ideas. Detail is added as a response to the simulations, after a mock up room is correctly sized and operations are tested. Other disciplines such as engineers, equipment planners, and interior designers participate at key points to offer solutions and to understand the impact of the future state on their contributions to the design. Decisions are structured to be made just in time instead of being based on traditional deliverables. Once these decisions are made about the design, production begins.

(Integrated Project Delivery) IPD: To facilitate comprehensive understanding of a project, enhance communication of all parties involved in creating and delivering a building, and to improve upon coordination challenges of traditional design, Lean-Led design often includes IPD. Integrated project delivery typically relies on some form of a single contract and close collaboration among all participants from concept through completion. These participants include the owner, architects, design disciplines, general contractor and often subcontractors at the outset. The bid and negotiation processes are interwoven with design, which eliminates the need to spend additional time on this step. IPD has been shown to increase efficiency, reducing the total time needed to complete the project. It also focuses the entire team on value to the end customer, which is not always the focus in traditional projects.

Move-in/ Post occupancy: Similar to traditional design, the operating procedures for key equipment are reviewed with the staff. Additionally, to increase standardization and efficiency, workplace organization is implemented, based on the Toyota 5s and visual workspace principles. The 5s acronym stands for Sort, Set in Order, Shine, Standardize and Sustain. In a healthcare facility, 5s can be applied to medication, supplies and equipment organization. Visual workspace organization creates well identified "homes" or locations for equipment, supplies and medications that are clear and consistent. Such careful pre-planning makes finding and replacing items simpler for staff. Workspace organization involves the staff in the placement of items, creating a smooth transition into the new space.

As healthcare looks to maximize every available fund with a focus on patient care, safety and works to eliminate waste, Lean-Driven Hospital design offers opportunities for healthcare facilities to understand and improve their work flow and processes to inform the design of their hospital. The result is a facility that is efficient, standardized and flexible. These features improve the ability of hospitals and staff to consistently provide excellent patient care, as well as continue to review and improve operations and processes in the future.

Keep improving!!

Made in the USA
Lexington, KY
10 March 2017